DISNEY

M⊙ANA

THE ESSENTIAL GUIDE

Written by
Barbara Bazaldua

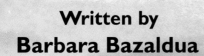

CONTENTS

Introduction 4

Moana 6

Motunui 8

Chief Tui 10

The village 12

Tapa and stories 14

Gramma Tala 16

Cavern of the wayfinders 18

Wayfinder ancestors 20

New voyages 22

What should Moana do?	24
Pua and Heihei	26
Moana's itinerary	28
Maui	30
Maui's fearless feats	32
The ocean	34
Maui's celebrity guide	36
Kakamora	38
On board!	40
Wayfinding tips and tricks!	42
Lalotai	44
Tamatoa	46
Shape-shifter!	48
Te Kā	50
Working together	52
Te Fiti	54
Escape from Lalotai!	56
Listen to your inner voice	58
How adventurous are you?	60
Moana's fleet	62
Acknowledgements	64

INTRODUCTION

A foreboding darkness threatens Moana's island home, and only she can stop it. But first she must convince a mischievous demigod to help her, battle sea monsters and – hardest of all – learn to trust her inner voice. It's a huge challenge. But the ocean has called Moana. And she is determined to answer.

MOANA

16-year-old Moana lives on Motunui island. As the chief's daughter, Moana knows she will one day lead her people. It's a big responsibility! This lively, intelligent girl wants to do what's right for her people, but she also needs to find out what's right for her.

Kind heart

Even as a little girl, Moana shows compassion by protecting a baby turtle as it crawls towards the sea. The ocean notices her kindness and approves.

Girl vs demigod

It takes confidence and a sense of humour to persuade a demigod to do what you want. Luckily, Moana has both!

HAVE YOU HEARD?

Moana's name means "ocean" in many Polynesian languages. It fits her perfectly!

Thrilling discovery

Moana is overjoyed to discover her ancestors were voyagers. Now she understands where her own longing to explore the ocean comes from.

Hair worn long and loose.

Shell necklace holds the heart of Te Fiti.

Tough going

On her voyage, sheer determination keeps Moana going however tough things get. She has a goal – and she's going to reach it!

Clothes made from tapa cloth and pandanus leaves.

TRUE OR FALSE?

Until she is chief, Moana has little to do all day.

*FALSE.
She advises farmers, fishermen and even the village cook!*

Ready for anything

Waves happen. So do volcanoes, giant crabs and difficult demigods. It's a good thing Moana is clever, fast-thinking and fearless or she would be sunk!

FUTURE CHIEF

Moana has taken part in village council meetings since she was eight. Her tall headdress shows she is the chief's daughter.

Strong, athletic body capable of steering for hours

1

Green riches

Motunui is covered in vegetation. About 40 kinds of plants and trees grow on the island, including taro, breadfruit and coconut palms. The villagers use coconut palms for everything from food to making rope.

Coconut palms provide food.

TRUE OR FALSE?

The people of Motunui hate drinking water from the coconut. It tastes too salty!

FALSE.
Coconut water actually tastes very sweet.

Home, sweet home

Moana's ancestors were wayfinders – travellers who sailed the ocean on big canoes, looking for new land. When they discovered Motunui, some of them settled here. Nowadays, the island provides everything that Moana and the villagers need to live.

Natural barrier

The coral reef that rings the island creates a calm lagoon of water for fishing and swimming. It also protects the island from crashing waves during storms. No one on Motunui is allowed to sail beyond the reef – the open sea is far too dangerous!

Cliff sides rise up into the clouds.

"The island gives us what we need!" Villagers

Golden sandy beach

MOTUNUI

The beautiful island of Motunui rises above the ocean waves like a green jewel. Steep, rocky mountains stretch high into the sky. Bright flowers and tumbling waterfalls lie around every corner!

Beautiful turquoise-coloured sea

CHIEF TUI

Chief Tui is a strong, responsible village leader who cares deeply about his people's safety. This demanding chief expects a lot from his daughter, Moana. Tui can be strict, but beneath his tough-guy shell, he is loving and kindhearted.

Firm but friendly expression

Necklace of whale teeth

CEREMONIAL DRESS

For important ceremonies Tui wears a headdress. He carries a special staff to signify his status.

HAVE YOU HEARD?

The red feathers which adorn Chief Tui's hut are a symbol of royalty.

Feathered red tapa-cloth skirt

Symbolic tattoos

Old secret

Chief Tui has a long-kept secret. Like Moana, he too once felt drawn to the ocean. But after a sad accident at sea, he decided to stay home on the island and do his duty – to lead, protect and care for his people.

> **"You are the future of your people, Moana."**
> Tui

Let's dance

Moana's mother, Sina, helps Tui to teach little Moana about the village and their people's customs. Sometimes leading everybody in dance together is the best method!

A lesson in stone

Standing at the top of the island's tallest peak, Tui tells Moana that someday she will be a great chief – and place her stone with those of her ancestors.

TRUE OR FALSE?

Chief Tui encourages his people to sail beyond the reef.

FALSE.
He believes the open ocean is very dangerous.

The home of a chief

Chief Tui's house is the largest in the village. It is built of wooden poles and beams, and thatched with palmetto leaves and grass.

THE VILLAGE

Moana's people have lived in the village for generations. Fed by freshwater streams from the mountains, the village is close to the lagoon for fishing, and also to the fields for growing crops.

Home sweet fale

The villagers' houses, called "fales", are made of wood with thatched roofs and no walls. Groups of families live together in each fale and share their home.

Daily life

Although the villagers work hard and have problems like everyone does, overall life is happy. They share everything from the fish they catch, to the baskets and cloth they weave. And when the work is done – they celebrate!

Canoes for fishing in the lagoon

TOOLS FOR EVERY TASK

Pound, dig, cut, slice, hook, stir… whatever needs to be done, Moana's people have a tool for the job. Tools are made from stone or bone, and fastened to wooden handles using plant fibres.

SPEAR
Thrown at fish, then hauled in with rope.

ADZE
Made in many sizes for cutting and carving wood.

Tall coconut tree

Line of fale buildings

Something's wrong

At first sight, the village may look perfect. But all is not well and the villagers begin to feel uneasy. The fish have disappeared from the lagoon, and the crops are rotting and turning black. What is going wrong?

Picture this

Tapa designs often show something that is important to the person who created the tapa. It's no surprise that little Moana paints a canoe on hers!

TAPA AND STORIES

For thousands of years, Oceanic people have created "tapa" – cloth made of tree bark. Every tapa tells a story. Some tapa have simple block-printed designs, while others are painted to tell great legends!

HAVE YOU HEARD?

Ancient tapa makers used dyes made from plants and even squid or octopus ink to create designs.

Trickster demigod Maui sets off to steal the powerful heart.

Maui prises away the heart with his fishhook.

The legend of Te Fiti's heart

Gramma Tala shows these action-packed tapa while she tells the legend of the mother island, Te Fiti. Te Fiti's heart had the power to create life, but it was stolen and lost 1,000 years ago. It is Moana's favourite story.

Trees die and darkness grows now that Te Fiti no longer has her heart.

TRUE OR FALSE?

After Maui steals the heart, he lives happily ever after.

FALSE. The heart falls into the sea. Maui loses his powers and disappears.

Demon of earth and fire, Te Kā, appears and strikes Maui from the sky.

GRAMMA TALA

Free-spirited Gramma Tala is happy to stand out from the crowd. The villagers consider her quirky but they like to listen to her tales. Tala is lovable and light-hearted, and shares a close bond with her granddaughter, Moana.

Hair decorated with bright red flower.

Precious heart
The ocean chose to wash up the heart of Te Fiti for Moana as a toddler. Gramma Tala has kept it safe for years and gives it to Moana now she is older.

Wise woman
Gramma Tala is wiser than the villagers realise. She keeps the knowledge of their ancestors' wayfinding alive, as well as legends and myths. Tala knows that the dying crops and fishless lagoon are caused by a growing darkness, that will drain all life from the island.

Clothes have manta ray patterns.

Walking stick helps her to get around.

> **"There is nowhere you could go that I won't be with you."** Gramma Tala

TRUE OR FALSE?
Gramma Tala's "animal guardian spirit" is a dolphin.

FALSE. It's a manta ray.

Storyteller

A lively storyteller, Gramma Tala entertains the village children with her stories. Little Moana believes every word is true!

HAVE YOU HEARD?

Gramma Tala listens to and trusts the ocean. She feels a special connection to it and loves dancing with the waves.

FAMILY HEIRLOOM

Tala's blue shell necklace once belonged to her wayfinder ancestors. She uses it to hold the heart of Te Fiti!

Words of encouragement

Tala is sure that Moana can find a way to restore Te Fiti's heart and save Motunui. Tala gives Moana her wayfinding necklace, so that Moana can keep the heart safely inside it during her journey.

CAVERN OF THE WAYFINDERS

In a far part of the island, there lies a secret cavern. The only way to reach it is on foot, through a hidden lava tube. Gramma Tala leads Moana there. She believes that it is time Moana learns the truth about their ancestors.

HAVE YOU HEARD?

Chief Tui knows that the boats are hidden in the cavern.

Sails ready to catch the wind again.

"What is this place?"
Moana to Gramma Tala

An amazing sight

Moana follows the lava tube into a vast cavern filled with enormous, ancient outrigger canoes. Their sails are unfurled as if waiting to catch the ocean winds once again.

Huge canoes tower over Moana.

Moana holds a torch to light her way.

Pool of water leads to waterfall.

Calling the ancestors

As Moana pounds a log drum, the pictures on the canoe sails begin to move, as if awakened by the sound.

Eyes fixed on new island spotted in the distance.

Strong muscles built by constant voyaging.

Clothing made from colourful island plants.

Matai Vasa in confident pose of a leader

WAYFINDER ANCESTORS

Moana's wayfinding ancestors voyaged thousands of miles in search of new islands, such as Motunui. Each island became a new home for some of them, who settled and raised families there.

> **"You really think our ancestors stayed within the reef?"** Gramma Tala to Moana

People of all ages took part in voyaging.

TRUE OR FALSE?
Matai Vasa's necklace is the same one Gramma Tala gives to Moana.

TRUE.
It has been handed down for generations.

Matai Vasa

Moana's first ancestor was Matai Vasa. The work of wayfinding made him and his people strong in spirit, mind and body. They knew who they were and what they could do.

Ocean escort

Dolphins leap near the canoe as it streaks through the water, much to the delight of the voyager children. They love watching the playful creatures!

All aboard

The ancestors' double-hulled canoes were big enough to carry dozens of people. They also held enough food and water for long voyages, and the plants and animals needed to settle on new islands.

21

Voyagers may not see the mountains of Motunui again for many months.

Villagers gather to bid the voyagers farewell.

NEW VOYAGES

The wayfinders who first settled on Motunui loved their home, but they still loved voyaging, too. There were so many more islands waiting to be discovered beyond the horizon!

Matai Vasa places his necklace on the new wayfinder leader.

Canoe is packed with supplies and ready to leave.

WHAT SHOULD MOANA DO?

Should Moana obey her father and stay at home? Or should she listen to Gramma Tala and make the perilous journey to restore the heart of Te Fiti? To make the right choice, Moana must listen to her own heart.

REASONS TO STAY

1. Dad says Gramma Tala's tales are just stories, and I shouldn't believe them.

2. Everyone else is content with their lives on our island. I should be happy, like them.

3. Dad tells me I will be a great chief if I just learn where I'm meant to be.

4. Everyone in the village believes it is dangerous to go beyond the reef. They can't all be wrong!

5. I fix people's roofs and hold their hands when they get a tattoo. They need me!

1. I've always felt a connection to the ocean. I can't ignore it. It must mean something.

2. My ancestors were great wayfinders. I really want to follow in their footsteps.

3. The ocean gave me the heart of Te Fiti. It must have chosen me to restore it and save my people.

4. Plants are dying – even the big banyan tree. Restoring Te Fiti's heart might be the only way to stop it happening.

5. I trust Gramma Tala and she thinks I should go. She says I have been chosen for the task and nobody else can do it!

PUA AND HEIHEI

The only thing adorable piglet Pua and confused rooster Heihei have in common is that Moana cares about them. Pua gives Moana endless love; Heihei gives her endless trouble. But she's kind and loyal to both!

Sweet vs scrappy

Cute, roly-poly Pua is happy, loyal and protective of Moana. Heihei is dimwitted, clueless and only thinks of himself!

Grey and white spotted coat

Soft ears made for petting.

Piglet overboard

When Pua joins Moana's first attempt to sail beyond the reef, he's swept overboard. Moana saves him, and his cheerful spirit isn't at all dampened by the experience.

Trusting trotter

Loyal, trusting Pua adores Moana and follows her everywhere like a dog. When Pua isn't trotting after Moana on his stumpy legs, he is chasing birds – although he never succeeds in catching them.

Trots on short legs and tiny feet.

Clumsy clucker

Heihei is always sticking his head where it doesn't belong – such as inside a coconut shell – and tripping over things.

Flashy red comb

> ## "There's more to Heihei than meets the eye..." Moana

Large eyes search for food (but he isn't good at successfully eating it)

Nothing to crow about

Heihei is not bright. In fact, this chippy chicken is about as intelligent as the coconut shells he's always getting his head stuck in!

HAVE YOU HEARD?

Ancient wayfinders took pigs and chickens on their voyages to discover and settle on new islands.

Sometimes trips over his own feet.

Troublesome stowaway

Heihei accidentally ends up on Moana's canoe and causes a lot of trouble on the journey. Moana always rescues Heihei, but he's too bird-brained to be grateful.

3
Give a speech
Convince Maui to help restore the heart of Te Fiti. Tell him he will be a hero again, as that may help.

4
Make a deal with a demigod
Strike a deal with Maui to help retrieve his fishhook so he can use its powers.

2
Find Maui
Follow Gramma Tala's instructions: sail towards the fishhook star constellation to find Maui.

1
Pack light
Before setting out, load canoe with food and water. Do NOT take Heihei. Oops – too late!

MOANA'S ITINERARY

Moana has a big challenge facing her if she is to restore the heart of Te Fiti and save the world from darkness. She needs to have a plan – and she's running out of time!

5

Visit Lalotai

Go to the realm of monsters, Lalotai. Get the fishhook back from monster crab Tamatoa.

6

Save the world

Get past lava monster Te Kā, restore the heart of Te Fiti and stop the darkness from spreading across the world.

7

Return home

Sail back home to Motunui (in triumph!) and reunite with Chief Tui, Sina and the villagers!

MAUI

Stealing Te Fiti's heart did not bring Maui the fame he craved. Instead, this demigod of wind and sea wound up exiled alone on a desolate island without his magic fishhook. It's been a long, lonely 1,000 years for loud, attention-seeking Maui!

Bad first impressions

Moana's first meeting with Maui goes badly. Maui thinks Moana is a fan, but when she demands his help he traps her in a cave and nabs her boat!

Tattoos represent his famous deeds.

Mission: fame

Moana tells Maui that if he helps her on her mission, he'll get his fishhook back, and be a big hero. He is convinced!

TRUE OR FALSE?

Maui is afraid of Te Fiti's heart when Moana reveals she has it.

TRUE.
He tells her it is cursed and will bring danger to them.

Lost and found

Maui needs his fishhook to regain his amazing shape-shifting powers. Once he has found it and got his powers back, he is able to appear to Moana in his favourite shape – a hawk.

Curved fishhook gives Maui shape-shifting powers.

Necklace made of pointed teeth.

"I know, not every day you get a chance to meet your hero." Maui

Big show-off

Maui boasts about all the awesome things he's done, but Moana learns that his confidence is just a cover. He secretly craves reassurance that he's okay just as he is.

MINI MAUI

This tattoo has his own opinions — he often acts as Maui's conscience. If Maui doesn't want to listen, he can push Mini Maui round onto his back!

Skirt of leaves from island plants

MAUI'S FEARLESS FEATS

Maui has been a very busy demigod. He has carried out some astonishing feats to make humans' lives better – and he likes to brag about them! He loves attention, but he also just wishes someone would remember to say "thank you".

Pulled up islands with his magic fishhook to give humans places to live.

STOLE FIRE and gave it to mortals to cook their food, light their homes and stay warm.

LASSOED THE SUN
to make it move more slowly and give humans longer days.

Harnessed the winds
to fill the sails of boats and shake food from the trees.

"I believe what you were trying to say... is thank you." Maui

RAISED THE SKY
so people could walk without bending over.

Defeated a monster eel
and buried its body in the sand. A tree sprouted and gave mortals the **coconut fruit.**

THE OCEAN

Moana has loved the ocean since she was young and longs to discover what lies beyond the reef. It's as if the ocean is calling to her like a friend. And when she ventures out at last, it guides and helps her on her journey.

A gift from the sea

The ocean offers Moana the heart of Te Fiti when she is a child. It chooses her to be the special person who will travel the seas and return the heart to its rightful owner.

Canoe sails across the lagoon.

Calm waves in the lagoon

What's out there?

Although the ocean looks calm and peaceful, it's also a place where storms rage and monsters lurk. Generations ago, Moana's ancestors believed the ocean united all lands and people. Now, the villagers are forbidden to venture too far out.

HAVE YOU HEARD?

Moana's first attempt to sail across the reef fails. But when she learns her people were wayfinders, she knows she must try again.

A little help here?

Churning storm waves capsize Moana's boat and toss her onto an empty beach. Isn't the ocean supposed to be helping her?! It is! It washes her up onto Maui's island.

Dark blue water lies beyond the reef.

"It chose me for a reason."
Moana on the ocean

Back onboard

No matter how many times Maui tosses Moana overboard, the ocean pops her back into the boat. Finally Maui gives up. The waves are obviously on Moana's side!

GREAT SWIMMERS

Squid swim tail first, tuna can dive 914m (3,000 ft) deep and swordfish zip along at 80kph (50 mph).

MAUI'S CELEBRITY GUIDE

It's not easy being a celebrity. It takes energy and dedication to keep your fans impressed. Just ask Maui. He's been wowing the crowds for thousands of years!

BE FRIENDLY TO FANS

Maui knows it can be overwhelming to meet him, so he's gracious about sharing his greatness with his fans. He never forgets to encourage them to thank him.

SHOW OFF WITH COOL STUNTS

Be the centre of attention wherever you go. Do some totally amazing tricks, like batting sea urchins in every direction, with just one blow of your fishhook!

PLAY UP YOUR STRENGTHS

Maui loves to stun fans with his supernatural strength. Breaking open a hidden entrance to the underworld with a big war cry is a sure way to do it!

DO DARING DEEDS

When you're a celebrity demigod, people expect you to take risks. Maui never lets his fans down. He's often the first to leap before he looks!

HOOK YOUR FANS

Fans love it when celebrities have special skills. Maui can shape-shift and fight with his magical fishhook. It's all part of his signature style!

"Maui always has time for his fans." Maui

37

KAKAMORA

The Kakamora sail the sea on their floating island, looking for the heart of Te Fiti. They will stop at nothing to get it! These pint-sized pirates might be small, but they strike fear into the hearts of everyone they meet.

> "Murdering little pirates." Maui

Boat surprise

Watch out! The Kakamora's floating island can be separated into a collection of boats. The pirates then surround and attack their victims from all sides.

Don't call them cute

Moana thinks the coconut-armoured Kakamora are cute. That is, until they launch spears tied to ropes at her canoe, and then zip-line onboard, with mayhem in mind!

Painted battle face to frighten foes.

Mighty mites

The Kakamora make weapons from bone, wood and other things they've salvaged or stolen. They will attack anyone who has something they desire, and they use their weapons with frightening speed and skill.

HAVE YOU HEARD?

An oar makes a good weapon against the Kakamora. Perfect for batting them away!

Heart snatchers

The Kakamora want the heart of Te Fiti. So when Heihei the chicken swallows it, the rascals grab him and swing back onto their boat. They don't expect Moana to follow them. No one has ever dared do that before!

Bone headdress creates warlike look.

Coconut hulls make tough armour.

Leaf wrappings protect wrists and ankles.

39

Float your boat

The outrigger works like a big float to keep the boat steady. Moana also stows Maui partly on the outrigger when he's paralysed by a dart!

ON BOARD!

Moana chooses a single-hulled outrigger canoe from the cavern of the ancestors for her journey across the open ocean. This strong, compact craft is the perfect size for Moana to set off by herself.

Rocking of boat makes holding on to rope a must.

TURTLE DESIGN

The sails of Motunui's fishing fleet are decorated with geometric tattoo patterns.

HAVE YOU HEARD?

Ancient double-hulled outriggers could carry up to 100 people. Moana's boat only holds her, a demigod and a rooster!

Hull and mast made of Koa wood shaped with stone adzes, chisels and files.

Paddle power

Outrigger canoes can be sailed or paddled. This means that Moana and Maui can keep moving, whatever the weather!

Pandanus leaf mats make a sturdy sail.

Strong ropes made from coconut fibres.

Paddle can also serve as rudder for steering.

Outrigger float built of light, buoyant wood.

WAYFINDING TIPS AND TRICKS!

Moana's ancestors sailed thousands of miles looking for new islands to settle on. Now it is Moana's turn to set sail... but she needs to learn a few things first!

HAVE YOU HEARD?

Ancient wayfinders did not use written maps. They memorised all the information they needed.

USE YOUR MIND

Wayfinding is more than just sailing. You must visualise where you are going in your mind. You need to remember where you have been before, so you can navigate to your new destination.

ROW YOUR BOAT

First, you have to leave the safety of your island's lagoon. That means getting past the reef and onto the open sea. Prepare to paddle – hard!

GET A GUIDE

If you can't tell a halyard from a half mast, find a teacher – like a demigod who knows his way around a wave!

CHECK THE CURRENT

Be aware of the direction of the current at all times. Stick your hand in the water to find out which way the water is flowing.

3 MORE TIPS!

1 Watch out for migrating seabirds. If it's the evening, they are flying towards land – but if it's morning, they are flying out to sea, looking for food.

2 If the bottom of the clouds look green, it means they are reflecting the colour of an island. Land ahead!

3 Never give up. A wayfinder doesn't quit!

MEASURE THE STARS

Check the position of the stars across the sky. Measuring their distance from the horizon can help orient you on the open ocean.

WATCH THE WEATHER

The sea may be calm, but watch the clouds and be aware of the wind. Big storms can blow up in minutes, and a wayfinder must always be prepared.

LALOTAI

A magical underworld of
wondrous beauty, Lalotai is the
home of legendary demons and
monsters. Few mortals have
ever been here, but this is
where Maui's fishhook is – and
Moana is determined to find it.

**Spiky
green fins**

**Monster is
ready to
attack.**

**Moana is
trapped in
monster's
long, sticky
tongue.**

**Strange
pink plant**

Pretty weird

Moana has never seen anything like Lalotai.
It's filled with creepy creatures, spooky
sounds, bristling spiny sea urchins, giant
anemone trees and underwater geysers
that blast unexpectedly on every side.

Take the plunge

The entrance to Lalotai is a swirling whirlpool at the bottom of a 1,000-foot-high cliff. All Moana has to do is jump in! At first she hesitates, but if Maui can dive in, so can she!

HAVE YOU HEARD?

Some sea creatures can create light. It's called "bioluminescence".

Welcome to my lair

Deep within Lalotai's glowing forest lies the lair of the monster Tamatoa. Few dare to enter this place – and even fewer return.

Beware of monsters

From scaly creatures to many-eyed beasts, the monsters of Lalotai are a frightening sight. Especially when they gobble one another up in a heartbeat!

TAMATOA

Grasping and greedy Tamatoa is a sinister scavenger who collects everything he finds. Once Tamatoa has his claws on something, this giant crab-monster is not about to let go!

Claw grabs Maui's fishhook.

Googly eyes stand out on stalks.

Pinned ya! Tamatoa traps Maui.

Unpleasant view

Mean Tamatoa loves to scare his victims. He uses one of his pincers to dangle them upside down, close to his grinning mouth and crooked teeth.

Shiny, sparkly hoard stuck to Tamatoa's back.

Bling-back crab

From treasures to junk, everything Tamatoa finds he wears on his 50-foot-wide back – including Maui's fishhook. Tamatoa thinks the bling makes him look beautiful!

"Watch me dazzle like a diamond in the rough."
Tamatoa

Moana holds out heart of Te Fiti.

Selfish shellfish

Tamatoa is huge and terrifying, but Moana finds the courage to stand up to him. She realises the crafty crustacean's weakness is greed – and uses the heart of Te Fiti to tempt him away from Maui.

SHAPE-SHIFTER!

With a just wave of his fishhook, Maui can swiftly change into any animal that he wishes! This incredible power is especially handy whenever he wants to do something that isn't possible in his human form.

NOT SO CONFIDENT

Maui has lost his confidence in his shape-shifting skills when he gets his fishhook back after 1,000 years. He tries to transform into a hawk, but instead he zaps himself from man to bug to pig to fish!

"YOU'RE LOOKING AT ME LIKE I HAVE A... SHARK HEAD."
MAUI

TINY BUT TRICKY

Being a bug has its advantages! Maui transforms into one in order to squeeze through a tiny crack in the rock and steal the heart of Te Fiti.

SHARK MAN

Maui makes a frightening shark with his toothy grin – but it's not as surprising as the time he accidentally transforms into a human with a shark's head! Moana thinks it's pretty funny.

MR GRUMPY GILLS

Having fins and gills might help in a swimming situation, but it's probably not much good for fighting the lava monster, Te Kā. No wonder Maui's fish face looks frustrated!

MIGHTY BIRD

As a hawk, Maui has razor-sharp talons and beak. He also boasts the ability to fly and dive through the air at the speed of the wind! His spectacular skills strike fear into any opponent.

TE KĀ

Te Kā is a mountain of red-hot lava and flame, surrounded by clouds of scalding steam and ash. The molten monster is by far the most dangerous foe Moana and Maui must face. But face it they must, if they are to reach the island of Te Fiti!

Blocked!

Moana sails, Maui flies, but they can't get past Te Kā to reach the barrier islands and Te Fiti. Te Kā's fiery fury blocks every attempt.

Scary and true

Chief Tui told Moana that Gramma Tala's tales about Te Kā were nonsense. They weren't! Te Kā is very real – but even bigger and scarier than in the stories.

"A demon of earth and fire!"
Gramma Tala on Te Kā

TRUE OR FALSE?

Te Kā wants Te Fiti's heart.

TRUE. And the monster will fight to get it!

Flames swirl around Te Kā's face.

Scorching air blasts from Te Kā's mouth.

Eyes glow with fiery fury.

Short reach

Te Kā strikes with flaming fists, hurls hot lava and causes tidal waves. If Moana and Maui are to get past it, they must exploit its one weakness: it can't move from the reef.

Fishhook disaster

Maui bravely battles Te Kā, but the fiery demon hits back hard, and cracks Maui's fishhook. Without it, Maui believes he is powerless and loses hope.

WORKING TOGETHER

Frustrated boat mates or true friends? Moana and Maui don't agree about anything at first, but as they face danger together, they learn that it takes two to make a team.

> "I got your back, Chosen One. Go save the world."
> **Maui**

FIRST IMPRESSIONS

Maui and Moana's first meeting doesn't go well. He thinks Moana is a foolish kid. She thinks he is a big loudmouth who has made a lot of trouble for everyone.

TAKING ON TE KĀ

Maui and Moana try to battle Te Kā as a team. Maui transforms into a hawk and attempts to hold the molten monster off, so Moana can sail past safely.

52

SHATTERED FRIENDSHIP

The duo's friendship seems broken. Maui's fishhook is badly cracked, and he blames Moana. She should have listened to him – because that's what pals do.

BEST OF FRIENDS

What do you call someone who helps you gain confidence, stay strong and most of all, believe in yourself? A best friend. That's what Maui and Moana become during their journey together.

SURPRISING EACH OTHER

It's a long climb up to the entrance of Lalotai. Maui is surprised by Moana's determination. He expected her to stay safely behind with the canoe on the beach!

TE FITI

Peaceful, loving Te Fiti is the mother island who generously gives life to the sea and the other islands. She is part island, and part spirit of life. When Te Fiti is happy, all is well!

Smiling, serene expression on face.

Creator of life

The tapa map shows islands forming around Te Fiti. She uses her heart to create life across the ocean. Moana must succeed in returning Te Fiti's heart, or destruction and decay will spread to these islands — and eventually the whole world!

Lush trees, vines and leaves form Te Fiti's hair.

Bountiful island

When Moana restores her heart, Te Fiti appears for a moment as a beautiful woman. She returns life to the land and the sea with a gracious gesture, then fades back into her island, which bursts into vivid bloom.

> **"Her heart held the greatest power ever known: it could create life itself."** Gramma Tala

HAVE YOU HEARD?
Te Fiti gives Moana a "hongi" greeting, by pressing their noses and foreheads together.

Te Fiti rises gracefully from the sea in the shape of a woman.

Act of bravery
It's not as simple to return the heart as Moana expects. She needs all her courage to take the final step.

BLOSSOM CROWN
Beautifully coloured flowers decorate the leafy crown on Te Fiti's head.

TRUE OR FALSE?
After greeting Moana and Maui, Te Fiti keeps Maui's broken fishhook.

FALSE.
She returns it to Maui – good as new!

Well, you're not even going to get *into* Lalotai then. Want to think again?

Can you outswim a snapping sea monster?

NO

YES

NO **YES**

Got a head for heights? Ready to jump into a giant whirlpool?

Are you taking care to stay near the bioluminescent plants so you can see where you're going?

NO

START

YES

ESCAPE FROM LALOTAI!

You're brave enough to enter Lalotai, but can you make it out? It's going to take skill and luck. Beware of tricky Tamatoa and hungry sea monsters on the way. Think fast!

YES

Can you sneak past Tamatoa the giant crab without him seeing you?

NO

Can you find a rock or something to hide behind? **NO**

OOPS! You've been caught by a sea monster!

YES

Well, now you're lost in the dark, where sea monsters lurk. You'll just have to run for it!

YAY! You've made it back safely to your canoe!

YES

Can you talk your way past Tamatoa without him realising?

NO

GULP! You've been eaten by Tamatoa!

LISTEN TO YOUR INNER VOICE

After Moana argues with Maui, she believes her quest is over and her efforts to return Te Fiti's heart have failed. Her confusion only ends when she listens to the voice inside her and finds the courage to keep going.

Ancestors' canoes glide on horizon.

Spirits of voyagers glow with blue light.

Finding Maui
When Maui loses his confidence, Moana tells him that there is more to him than just his great deeds or his reputation. She encourages him to listen to his own inner voice.

A spirit guide
A glowing, ghostly manta ray circles Moana's canoe. It is the spirit of Gramma Tala, come to help Moana continue her journey of self-discovery.

Heart of courage
The ancestors' singing and Gramma Tala's words help Moana trust her inner voice again. With true courage, she dives deep beneath the waves to retrieve the heart of Te Fiti.

> ## "Nothing on earth can silence the quiet voice still inside you."
> **Gramma Tala**

Moana is comforted by her grandmother.

Gramma Tala's spirit takes on human form.

HAVE YOU HEARD?

Manta rays represent great strength and wisdom in many Pacific Island cultures.

Words of wisdom

Feeling defeated, Moana gives the heart back to the ocean. She thinks she is not the right person to return it to Te Fiti. But the words of Gramma Tala's spirit and the song of her wayfinder ancestors soon help Moana to regain her self belief.

59

HOW ADVENTUROUS ARE YOU?

Some people will go anywhere and try anything, while others are more cautious and like to plan ahead. How adventurous are you? Take this quiz to find out!

1
DO YOU DREAM OF JOURNEYING TO FARAWAY PLACES?

A) I prefer to stay home with family and friends.
B) I can't wait to go! Where's my boat?
C) Only if my fans will be there.
D) What's a faraway place? Is there food?

2
WHAT KIND OF STORIES DO YOU LIKE MOST?

A) Stories about my family.
B) Stories about exploring.
C) Stories about myself.
D) Stories told while I'm enjoying a snack.

3

WHO DO YOU WANT TO BE SOMEDAY?

A) A leader.
B) I'm still figuring it out.
C) A superstar.
D) I've never thought about it.

5

WHAT ANNOYS YOU MOST?

A) Being argued with.
B) Being told I shouldn't try to do something.
C) Being ignored.
D) Being hungry.

4

IF YOU COULD SHAPE-SHIFT INTO ONE CREATURE, WHAT WOULD YOU BE?

A) A dog. They're loyal and dependable.
B) A dolphin so I could explore the sea.
C) Why limit myself to just one?
D) A delicious bug. Oh wait. Maybe not!

MOSTLY As – CHIEF TUI

Responsible

You like staying close to home and sharing adventures with family and friends. You're careful and caring, and always make sure everyone is having fun.

MOSTLY Bs – MOANA

Brave

You're like Moana. You see the world as one big place to explore. The horizon beckons. But your biggest adventure will be discovering what's inside you.

MOSTLY Cs – MAUI

Fame-seeking

You love attention, and you'll dare to try almost anything to get it. Be careful! Sometimes it's better to look before you leap.

MOSTLY Ds – HEIHEI

Hungry

You're always thinking about food and sometimes you end up on adventures you weren't planning to have. Pack snacks and stay focused!

MOANA'S FLEET

Thanks to Moana, the people of Motunui have rediscovered their heritage as wayfinders. They will always love their island, but Moana has given them the joy and freedom of the waves, wind and far horizons to explore.

Chief Tui stands on the prow of a canoe.

A fleet of joyful villagers.

Gramma Tala's spirit ray joins the celebration.

A true leader

Moana adds the conch shell that the ocean gave her to her ancestors' stone pile. She has proven herself as a brave leader and found her place at last.

"I may have gone a little ways past the reef." Moana

Maui honours Moana with a swift visit.

Even little Pua can ride the waves.

Farewell to darkness
Not only has Moana stopped the darkness, her courage has healed the tension between herself and her father. Her example has shown Tui and her people who they are and who they can be.

ACKNOWLEDGEMENTS

 Penguin Random House

Editor Ruth Amos
Senior Designer Lynne Moulding
Additional Editors Julia March, Lauren Nesworthy
Design Assistant Lisa Rogers
Pre-Production Producer Siu Yin Chan
Producer Zara Markland
Managing Editor Sadie Smith
Design Manager Ron Stobbart
Art Director Lisa Lanzarini
Publisher Julie Ferris
Publishing Director Simon Beecroft

First published in Great Britain in 2016 by
Dorling Kindersley Limited
80 Strand, London WC2R 0RL
A Penguin Random House Company

10 9 8 7 6 5 4 3 2 1
001-280595-Oct/16

Page design copyright © 2016 Dorling Kindersley Limited

A CIP catalogue record for this book
is available from the British Library.

ISBN: 978-0-24123-229-3

Printed in Slovakia.

DK would like to thank Kathryn Boynton for
design assistance, and Chelsea Alon, Rima Simonian,
Laura Hitchcock, Heather Knowles, Grace Lee,
Jeff Clark and Tony Fejeran at Disney Publishing.

A WORLD OF IDEAS
SEE ALL THERE IS TO KNOW

Discover more at
www.dk.com
www.disney.com